D1134781

You're my friend
so I
brought you
this book

You're my friend so I brought you this book

Edited & Introduced by
John Marvin

STANYAN BOOKS

RANDOM HOUSE

For Lee Mendleson

This is a book about friendship,
and so it is a book about love.
Further, it is a book of under-
standing and misunderstandings.

Nothing is more precious than
a friend and yet we take our
friends for granted. Nothing is
more helpful than a friend's help.

This book was made to help your
friendships along.

John Marvin, 1970

I find as I grow older that I love
those most whom I loved first.

Thomas Jefferson

All things rest in heaven when
you sleep beside a friend.

Paul Ryder

Let no man grumble when his
friends fall off; instead let him
go to the coffee house and
take another.

Lord Byron

I have made generous provision in my will for all of my friends. For instance, Sam will get the Doberman pinscher and Carl and Bill share equally in my aluminum watch chain.

W. C. Fields

Follow your friends to hell and your reward will be a place with them.

Alexander Drey

Doubtless, you want to be my friend. Come back on Tuesday.

Dorothy Parker

I have room for one more friend
and he is everyman.

Woody Guthrie

Friendship exists only when men
harmonize in their views of things
human and divine.

Cicero

We need the whole world as
a friend.

Herbert Hoover

Even the ability to hate demands
a certain kind of friendship.

Franklin D. Roosevelt

Today I am still close to you in
spirit—a little your friend, because
I withhold nothing from you.

Albert Camus

Being a friend to dogs and men
is a good day's work.

Bevins Jay

I am wealthy in my friends.

Shakespeare

True friendship is a plant of slow growth.

George Washington

I fanned the flame of friendship and it fired love.

Alexander Drey

Love begets respect and friendship surely follows.

Jean Cocteau

If I don't have friends, then I ain't got nothin'.

Billie Holiday

Must I travel all the world alone, or will you be my friend?

Christopher Flovio

Offering our hands in friendship, we expect nothing in return; therefore, it should come as no surprise when we get back friendship. It follows that people give like and get like.

Hon. R. D. Miller

Friendship demands the ability to do without it.

Ralph Waldo Emerson

A friend lay dying and I could have said "raise your head a little and I'll try to show you Spain," but he slipped away and I'll never have the chance again.

Rod McKuen

My friends are lazy today, considering the fact that I'm dying — they might have sent a card.

Rudyard Kipling

Out of uniform, he was just my friend.

Douglas MacArthur

Funny you should like me, I only know you as a friend.

Oscar Wilde

As friends, we don't see eye to eye, but then we don't hear ear to ear either.

Buster Keaton

All we need to make the day go better is to remember our friends, or maybe one friend's face.

Bessie Lorraine Boles

Friendship ruins angels and elevates men.

Alexander Drey

Don't talk of friendship, send roses.

Karl Enohpelet

Friendship needs care.

Richard Nixon

Friendship needs feeding.

John Nance Garner

Whenever there is friendship, there's a chance for human beings.

Alexander Pope

Sometimes I feel I haven't any friends but my enemies more than make up for missing friendships.

Judy Garland

Fight off my friendly advances, but you do so at your peril.

Corrine LeMay

Let the soul be assured that somewhere in the universe, it should rejoin its friend.

Ralph Waldo Emerson

True friendship exhibits itself more in solitude than in the presence of others.

Rousseau

A king cannot have a friend, a peasant can.

Benjamin Franklin

Take care with the beginning of
friendship—for the end will
always manage itself.

James Lytton

Beware of the friend who has
all of the answers but none
of the questions.

Voltaire

I do not give lectures or
a little charity. When I
give, I give myself.

Walt Whitman

Friends make good furniture
and easy windows.

Constance Nivelle

People are lonely because they
build walls instead of bridges.

Joseph Newton

That son of a bitch summer is
coming and I need a friend.

Bevins Jay

Friendship bridges the gap
between what things are and
what they could be.

Roger Holmes

Quarrel with a friend — and you both are wrong.

Lao-tse

True friendship brings sunshine
to the shade, and shade
to the sunshine.

Thomas Burke

Friendship is a horizon—which
expands whenever we approach it.

E. R. Hazlip

I recreate in a friend my own
world—or take to me his new
one—and we two look at one
mirror from different sides.

Friedrich Emerson

I am feeding my friends beans
with pork, I expect some will
not stay for dinner.

Gertrude Stein

There's always something about your success that displeases even your best friends.

Mark Twain

Laughter is not a bad beginning for friendship, and it is the best ending for one.

Oscar Wilde

Friendships last when each friend thinks he has a slight superiority over the other.

Balzac

If I cannot be your friend, I suppose I'll have to content myself with being your lover.

Rod McKuen

A prudent enemy is preferable to a friend without discretion.

Jean de La Fontaine

Do not bore me with your petty attempts at friendship. I have owned a dog who licked my face, and a man I never knew died for me a world away.

Ellen Hawthorn ·

He who gives up a friendship
for ambition burns a picture
to obtain the ashes.

Arabic Proverb

Friendship is not made by a
crisis — it is only revealed by it.

Mark Adams

A friend is a present
you give yourself.

Robert Louis Stevenson

False friends are a form of self-flagellation.

Karl Marx

A friend can ride you on his shoulders by telling you the truth.

Terrance Wilde

What a fiend you are, you must be someone's friend.

Felicity O'Brian

He is my friend and he is me.

Abraham Lincoln

Show me the man who is your friend and I will know what your ideal of manhood is—and what kind of man you yourself wish to be.

William Carlyle

Love must constantly test its techniques and measures—but friendship has its own vitality.

William Longacre

The world is my country, and all mankind are my brethren.

Thomas Paine

My friend loves all the blotches
on my back, even those not
made by love.

Rod McKuen

Free me from false lovers,
bind me to true friends.

Amy Lowell

I fired the butler when he
became my friend.

Charles Laughton

Front or back, aged or young,
wise or petty, I love my friends.
But they must never know.

Cole Porter

Love without friendship is like a shadow without the sun.

Japanese Proverb

What is a friend? A single soul which dwells in two bodies.

Aristotle

Memory is the enemy of friendship.

John Milton

Never trust a friend who deserts you at a pinch.

Aesop

I am thinking of firing my friends and hiring only lovers from here on in. Of late they are more presentable and less trouble.

Alexander Drey

The most I can do for my friend is simply to be his friend. I have no wealth to bestow on him. If he knows that I am happy in loving him, he will want no other reward. Is not friendship divine in this?

Henry David Thoreau

Face your friends and you turn your back on adversity.

Richard Burton

He that is not with me
is against me.

St. Luke

Every friend is a possible temptation.

W. R. Nelson

What a friend we have in Jesus.

From an old hymn

There is magic in the memory
of a schoolboy friendship;
it softens the heart, and even
affects the nervous system of
those who have no hearts.

Benjamin Disraeli

My friends are few, but altogether sufficient.

Winston Churchill

To be a good friend, it helps to be a genius.

John F. Kennedy

Labor not to make friends, they will come in the dead of night without your bidding.

Sister Hazlett

Friendship? Yes, please.

Charles Dickens

Of that short roll of friends written in my heart, your name begins.

John Donne

An enemy should be hated only as much as one may be hated who could one day be a friend.

Sophocles

You should not try my friendship as you should not try my love.

Jack Fitzgerald

If you're my friend, then take me to bed and cover me with kisses. That is something all my lovers hesitate in doing.

Romona Sanchez

Raise the bridge, my friend is sailing by.

St. Augustine

If I had one friend, I had a million—but that was 1953.

Jack Kerouac

Now that you have gained my confidence, you might just as well take title to my friendship.

Gordon Crawford

I love you. Please don't let that stand in the way of our friendship.

Roy Fitzgerald

War is killing off the friendship of man for man.

Thomas Middleton

I have two and one half friends
and you are not one of them.

Ian Fleming

The antidote for fifty enemies
is one friend.

Aristotle

It is better to have your friends
learn of your faults than
your enemies.

Persius

Yes, he is a thief. Yesterday he stole a chicken and a loaf of bread. But I forgive him, he is the only friend I've got.

Romany Speare

Fly the flag of friendship or you'll stumble over love.

Alexander Drey

Don't blame my wife because we are no longer friends. Blame your wife.

Fred Allen

Tell him he can send his friendship to Cleveland. They can use it there.

W. C. Fields

Funny, you don't look like a
friend—ah, but they never do.

Grace Metalious

Open your heart to a friend and
you close that door to love.

Herbert Moran

If I stop killing your chickens,
can we be friends?

Bob Burns

It is a fine
friendship
that asks nothing
and gets it.

Benson Drew

Friendship has so much of
sovereignty and of religion too,
that no prescription can
be written against it.

John Donne

Chimairis was my friend until
she bit my belly.

Pierre Lougs

Imitating Christ is opening
the door to friendship.

Billy Graham

I like your dog, but I am not sure
that will help us to be friends.

Tyrone Power

Hey, friend, wake up, I'm
throwing rocks at
your windowpane.

Scott MacKenzie

Be slow in choosing a friend,
slower in changing.

Benjamin Franklin

A friend follows you into
adversity and emerges with
you to prosperity.

Arthur B. Hays

We have lost our sense of
values: When your fence falls
you mend it, when your
friendship fails you run.

Hawthorne

Of late, I have no friends; I must be doing something right.

Somerset Maugham

A fine friend you turned out to be.

Oliver Hardy

Please believe me, I never wanted your friendship; you forced it on me.
But thank you all the same.

Chevio Meridith

I get by with a little help

from my friends.

John Lennon/Paul McCartney

There is a chance we may be friends, but I will have to stop loving you in order to concentrate on that aspect of our relationship.

Roy Scheer

I am your friend, accept no substitutes.

Groucho Marx

Come, my friend, I'll take you boating and later to a house of joy.

Jean Genet

So sleep my friend
into the dawn
for all the warm
and gentle girls
have come along and gone.

Rod McKuen